Santorini in 3 Days

This is a three days-2-nights guide to Santorini, with a perfect 72 hours plan that will guide you on the best way to enjoy this fantastic Greek island. All tips, maps, costs, information, are included so that you feel like you have your best friend with you showing you around this marvelous place.

This guide has been created by the travel bloggers team of Guidora, after visiting the Santorini island for several times and experiencing first hand the best that this island has to offer.

The information provided can also cater for travelers who want to spend more than three nights in Santorini. All the suggestions for restaurants and hotels are our own and we have tried to take under consideration a medium budget for most of them.

Table of Contents

Introduction

Santorini is an island in the southern Aegean Sea, about 200 km (120 mi) southeast of Greece's mainland. The total Santorini's land area is 90.623 km2 (34.990 sq mi). Santorini is essentially what remained after an enormous volcanic explosion that destroyed the earliest settlements on a formerly single island and created the current geological caldera. The population of the island is about 16,000 inhabitants. The municipality of Santorini comprises the inhabited islands of Santorini and Therasia and the uninhabited islands of Nea Kameni (Volcano), Palaia Kameni, Aspronisi, and Christiana.

View of the volcanic caldera cliffs

The caldera side (west coast) of the terrain is rocky, with unusual rock formations. Other areas have a gentler terrain.

The volcanic caldera cliffs

The climate is moist. The summer is warm with cool evenings, especially in August when the famous 'Meltemia' winds are present.

The architecture is typical Cycladic (white houses with blue windows and doors). However, in Santorini, you may also see the Cave Houses dug into the volcanic rock. The Capital of the island is **Fira**, which is built on the Caldera cliffs on the west coast.

Santorini remains the home of a small, but flourishing, **wine** industry, based on the indigenous grape varieties, *"Assyrtiko," "Athiri"* and *"Aidani."* The viticulture pride of the island is the sweet and vigorous *Vinsanto*, a dessert wine made from the best sun-dried Assyrtiko, Athiri, and Aidani grapes. You may also taste white wines that are extremely dry with a strong, citrus scent and mineral and iodide salt aromas contributed by the ashy volcanic soil.

Other local specialties are *melitinia* (a dessert with cheese which is prepared during the Easter period), *Brantada* (codfish with potatoes), *koskosela* (scrambled eggs with vegetables and cheese), *sfouggato* (traditional pie with courgettes) and *tomato croquettes*.
zucchini:

How to Get to Santorini by Ferry or Flight

There are two ways to get to Santorini from Athens: By flying with Aegean, Olympic Air or Ryanair and by getting a ferry, either the slow one (9 hours) or the quick one (4.5 hours). If you ask yourself if you should be using a flight or a ferry, read through for all the details, costs and information on these options.

1.Flying from Athens to Santorini
Flying from Athens to Santorini is, of course, the fastest route and the flight from Athens International Airport to the Santorini Airport, takes about 40 minutes and it has no stops. Six airline companies have frequent flights on this route, especially during the busy summertime: Aegean Airlines, Olympic Air (this is now the same company with Aegean Airlines), Ryanair, Ellinair, Skyexpress, and Volotea. The best three companies to fly with are Aegean Airlines, Olympic Air and then Ryanair.

The best one out of the three is by far Aegean Airlines: they are very punctual, their airplanes have the most comfortable seats, and they have the best service. Albeit, Aegean Airlines is usually the most expensive one to fly with.

The cost of a flight ticket from Athens to Santorini can vary from a mere 30 euros if you book early enough with Ryanair, to 150 euros if you book last minute with Aegean. Usually, a one-way ticket should cost around 80-90 euros.

The airport code of Santorini is <u>JTR.</u> Please bear in mind that Santorini is also called "Thira" or "Thira Island," so you may find it under this name in some flight search engines. The airport code of Athens Airport is <u>ATH.</u> You can use the local website <u>www.viva.gr</u> to find and book your flights – it is well designed and very functional. Alternatively, you can book via the websites of the airline companies.

Airlines that Fly to Santorini
Here are the sites of the six airlines that fly from Athens to Santorini:
Aegean Airlines: <u>http://en.aegeanair.com</u>
Olympic Air: <u>https://www.olympicair.com/en</u>
Ryanair: <u>www.ryanair.com</u>
Ellinair: <u>http://en.ellinair.com</u>
Skyexpress: <u>http://www.skyexpress.gr</u>
Volotea: <u>http://www.volotea.com</u>

Tips about your flight from Athens to Santorini
a. The airplanes are small, and they don't have a turbine. You cannot carry too big carry-ons inside, and they get a little bumpy on the air sometimes. Don't worry; they are very safe. Here is an airplane you may fly with:

b. The Airport of Santorini is tiny and not well organized. It has poor air condition and not a lot of shops. The little size of the airport and the lack of stores will be more critical for your return flight, if you need to wait, e.g. for one hour in the airport, you may have to "hunt" for a seat. One of the good things is of course that you don't need a bus to get from the airplane to the airport.

c. The Airport of Santorini is 4-5 km from the main village of Santorini that is called Fira. If you get a taxi, you should expect to pay around 10-15 euros to get from the airport to Fira and approximately 20 euros to get from the airport of Santorini to Oia.

2. Getting a Ferry from Athens to Santorini
If you plan to use a ferry to go from Athens to Santorini, you should know that there are two different ports to take the ship, the **Piraeus** port, and the **Rafina** Port. Moreover, there are two distinct kinds of ships you can get, the slow one (around 9 hours) and the fast and more expensive one, which will take you up to 4.5 hours.

Here is a map of where are the ports of Piraeus and Rafina, in correlation with the Athens International Airport and the center of Athens.

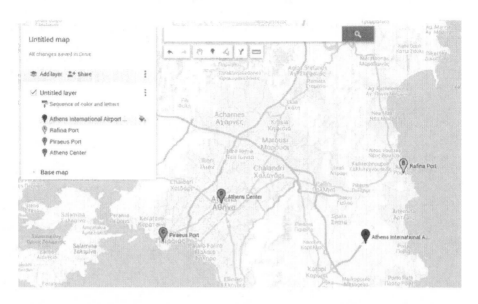

Frequently Asked Questions about Using a Ferry to get from Athens to Santorini

Q: How long is the ferry ride from Athens to Santorini? From 4.5 hours to 8 hours, depending on the ferry you are taking.

Q: How much is the ferry from Athens to Santorini? From 40 euros to 70 euros per person one way.

Q: What is the Athens to Santorini Ferry Timetable? Check it out at www.viva.gr

Q: Is there an Athens to Santorini Overnight Ferry? No, there isn't one.

Q: Can I get a car on the boat/ferry? In some ferries, yes. Not in all type of ferries, so please pay attention when you are booking.

Q: Where can I book a ticket for a ferry? You can do it at www.viva.gr. Please bear in mind that these are not electronic tickets so you will have to pick them up at a particular location or have them sent to you.

Read a more detailed explanation below:

a. Getting the Ferry from Piraeus Port to Santorini

To go to Piraeus, you can use the electric train which crosses the city of Athens, and you should stop at the final destination. If you arrive at the Athens airport, take the X96 Bus. It departs every 20' from the airport bus station, and it takes about 70' to reach the port. If you take a taxi from the airport to the port, it should cost, about 35€. Otherwise, if you get the taxi from any other part of Athens, it should cost you about 15-20€.

In the example below, you can see the itineraries and the prices of ferries leaving from Piraeus port to Santorini. You will find that there are ferries that will get you in Santorini at almost 5 hours with 55 euros and others that are a little bit cheaper, at 40 euros and will get you to Santorini at 7.5 hours (or usually 8.5 hours).

Piraeus to Santorini Ferries Itinerary.

b. Getting the Ferry from Rafina's Port to Santorini.

Rafina is a town with a port, and it is the second biggest port of Athens second to Piraeus harbor. Rafina is 30kms outside of Athens. To go to Rafina, you can use the bus from *Mavromateon Street – Pedion Areos* (it is a 10minutes walk from the central train station Victoria). The bus departs every 15'-45' starting from 05.45am and until 22.30pm. It takes 1h to take you to the Piraeus Port, and the ticket costs 2,40€.

Going from the Airport of Athens to Rafina's Port: If you arrive at Eleftherios Venizelos airport, and you want to go to the Rafina port, you can take the bus; it takes 30 minutes and it costs 3€:

Taxi from Athens to Rafina's Port: You can also get a Taxi from the Athens center to Rafina's port. It takes almost 1h (depends on the traffic), and it costs about 35€.

Ferries Itinerary from Rafina to Santorini

How to Arrive in Santorini (Extra Information & Timetables)

-By airplane
Daily direct flights from the *Athens International Airport 'Eleftherios Venizelos'* to Santorini –the flight duration is 40'. Two airline companies fly to Santorini directly from Athens: Aegean Airlines (which is the same company with Olympic Airlines) and Ryanair.

Charter flights to the Greek island from many €pean cities such as Rome, Budapest, and Vienna. These charter flights start in April and end in October. The distance from the airport of Santorini to the main city of the island, Fira, is about 5km.

-By ship
From *Piraeus* Port (Attica's biggest port) or *Rafina Port, which is 30kms outside of Athens.* To go to Piraeus, you can use the electric train which crosses the city of Athens, and you should stop at the final destination. If you arrive at the Athens airport, take the X96 Bus. It departs every 20' from the airport bus station, and it takes about 70' to reach the port.

If you take a taxi from the airport to the port, it should cost you about 35€. Otherwise, if you get the taxi from any other part of Athens, it should cost you about 15-20€. To go to Rafina, you can use the bus from *Mavromateon Street – Pedio Areos* (it is a 10minutes walk from the central train station Victoria). The bus departs every 15'-45' starting from 05.45am and until 22.30pm. It takes 1h to take you to the Piraeus Port, and the ticket costs 2,40€.

11

If you arrive at Eleftherios Venizelos airport, and you want to go to the Rafina port, you can take the bus; it takes 30' and it costs 3€:

Eleftherios Venizelos Airport to Rafina Bus Timetable
Monday to Sunday: 04:40, 05:35, 06:10, 07:05, 08:50, 10:30, 12:20, 13:20, 14:10, 15:20, 16:30, 18:00, 19:20, 20:45, 22:20

Please notice that the times might change, so you should also consult online the bus schedule before planning your trip.

Taxi: You can also get a Taxi from the Athens center to Rafina's port. It takes almost 1h (depends on the traffic), and it costs about 35€.

Here is a map that shows where is Rafina Port, the Athens International Airport, which is also called "Eleftherios Venizelos Airport," Piraeus Port and the center of Athens.

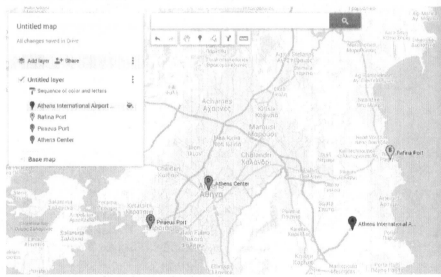

Get This Map Online: http://bit.ly/athensports

Useful Telephones and Travel Information
Athens International airport (El. Venizelos): +30 210 3530000, www.aia.gr
Santorini Airport: +30 22860 28400 Departures-arrivals: +30 22860 28702
Port Authorities: +30 22860 22239
Buses: +30 22860 25404 & 25462
Radio taxis (taxi stand/Fira): +30 22860 22555
Cable car: +30 22860 22977 & 22978
Greek National Tourist Organization Office: +30 22860 27199
Car Rental Association, Tel.: +30 22860 71200
Motorbike Rental Association, Tel.: +30 22860 22801
Health Center (Fira): +30 22863 60300
Post Office (Fira): +30 22860 22238

Santorini's Buses Timetable:
You can get it at http://ktel-santorini.gr/ktel/images/pdfs/ktel.pdf

Banks: Open from Monday to Friday 08.00-14.00pm. Located on the main square of Fira and the road from Fira to the port. ATMs are everywhere.

Credit Cards: Internationally recognized credit cards are accepted at restaurants and shops.

GMT: Time zone in Greece is GMT+2

Where to Stay in Santorini

Our favorite hotel recommendation for Santorini is the **Agnadema Apartments** *and the whole three days' itinerary is based on that.* However, if you prefer to stay in another place, you can find a complete guide on the next section, on the best villages to stay at in Santorini and the best hotels in these villages. You can also follow the same three days' itinerary plan if you choose to stay at any other hotel in Santorini. Guidora does not have any affiliation with any of these hotels.

Having said that here is a photo of the **Agnadema Apartments** in Firostefani village in Santorini:

Address: Firostefani, 84 700, Santorini Island
Tel.: +30 22860 25284; agnadema@otenet.gr
Link: http://bit.ly/Agnadema
Price per night: 120€ (130$) for a double room (depends on the period you are going to travel to Santorini- In August, the hotel may cost much more)
Recommended: Spacious and clean rooms with private balcony and an amazing view of the Aegean Sea, Thirasia Island, and the volcano.
Book it Online: http://bit.ly/Agnadema

Where to Stay in Santorini (Detailed Guide)

Here is a small guide for you to help you get the best possible place and hotel to stay according to how you want to enjoy the island.

The Best Villages to Stay in Santorini

There are four main places where visitors stay in Santorini: Fira Village (the capital), Imerovigli Village (close to Fira), Oia (fantastic sunset) and Perissa (black beach, cheaper place to stay). Here are the pros and cons of each site:

Fira

Fira is the most prominent village of Santorini Island; it has a lot of people ranging from youngsters who want to party in the clubs of the village, to couples who enjoy the scenic views of the caldera and the fabulous restaurants and hotels. It doesn't have a beach, and you will have to drive 10kms to get to a decent beach to swim. Fira village is built on the hill, and it offers a fantastic experience. It is quite expensive, and if you want to stay close to Fira village with a lower price, you will have to go to "Karterados" Village, which is 3-4 km away from it. Of course, you will have to drive to Fira every night (or get the bus), and you have to know that you will have to leave your car at the parking in the entrance of Fira and walk on foot (about 500m). Fira offers five 5-star hotels and fifteen 4-star hotels.

Imerovigli

Close to Fira, Imerovigli is also built on the caldera hill and offers fantastic views. It is less crowded than Fira, and usually, couples go there. It doesn't provide a beach, and it's not for young people who want to party. It is romantic, with white houses and fabulous hotels. Imerovigli offers six 5-star hotels and ten 4-star hotels.

Oia

Oia is well known all over the world for its fantastic sunset. It is also a beautiful village with excellent small white houses and famous restaurants. Oia is quite expensive to stay, though. It doesn't offer any great beach to swim, and you will have to drive through a tiny and crowded road to get to Fira in the evening. Oia has 13 5-star hotels and seven 4-star hotels. Apparently, it is the most luxurious village in Santorini.

Perissa Village

Perissa is the cheapest place to stay in Santorini island. It offers the vast black beach (at least 5kms of the black sanded beach) and many great beach bars where you can relax and enjoy yourself. It doesn't offer any scenic views, and the village is nothing special regarding architecture and beauty.

FREQUENTLY ASKED QUESTIONS ABOUT WHERE TO STAY IN SANTORINI

– Where to Stay in Santorini to Party?
You should stay in Fira Village. It is the most crowded place, with many bars and nightclubs. All the young people stay here, or close to Fira. If you don't have the budget to stay inside Fira, try to stay in Karterados village, which is 4kms away.

- Where to Stay in Santorini on Honeymoon?
You should stay either in Oia village or Imerovigli. You can visit Fira just for the views, but you will have a much more relaxed honeymoon if you stay at Oia or Imerovigli. The first choice would be Oia village in that case.

– What is the Most Expensive Area to Stay in Santorini?
Oia Village and Fira Village are the most expensive areas to stay in Santorini

– What are the cheapest areas to Stay in Santorini?
Kamari Village and Perissa village are the most affordable areas to stay in Santorini.

– Should I use Airbnb to stay in Santorini?
You could try Airbnb for your stay in Santorini, but you will not find any significant opportunities. Prices are high in Airbnb as well. Especially in July, August, and September that are the peak months for Santorini.

– Can I find a fantastic hotel with 50E per night in Santorini?
No. You cannot. If you go to Santorini in August and September, you should plan for a budget of 120E to 150E per night for a double room, as the minimum to get a beautiful scenic view to the caldera. With 50E per night, you can stay in small, everyday rooms outside of Fira, usually at Perissa or Kamari.

- Where to Stay in Santorini on a Budget?
If you are on a budget, the cheapest double room you can find in July/August is usually 40 to 50 euros for very basic accommodation. No views, no breakfast and hopefully a clean room. You should avoid searching the villages of Oia, Imerovigli and the center of Fira for this type of budget accommodation and look at villages such as Vlychada, Perissa or Vorthos (a couple of km away from the airport of Santorini). Unfortunately, we cannot recommend you any decent room at this price. We have stayed at more than 10 of them during the past years, but they are the basic type of accommodation.

-Where are Santorini's best views?
You can enjoy the best views of Santorini from 3 places: From **Fira** village, from **Imerovigli** village and **Oia** village. Of course, as Santorini is a volcano island, you should be on the edge of the caldera to get these fantastic views, which made this little gem island worldwide famous.

– Is it dangerous to drive in Santorini?
Santorini is a volcano island. The roads are tiny and with bad lighting in the evening. It has many scooters, many cars, and many other strange vehicles on the road at every time of the day. We cannot say it is dangerous, as the speeds are low, but certainly, it is not a breeze to drive in Santorini. You should always take care.

– Are the rooms Big enough in the Hotels in Santorini?
No, they are not.The land is expensive on a volcano island, so don't expect to get US size hotel rooms. The baths are usually small, and the rooms are just ok to fit in a double bed with some extra space. Of course, they make it up for you with the fantastic balconies that offer scenic views of the caldera.

– Anything I should be aware of before booking a hotel in Santorini?
You should know that sometimes, there is a strange smell coming from the volcano, which no one can do something about. So, you may find yourself in a situation where you have a fantastic view of the caldera and a strange smell coming to you from the air. Unfortunately, you cannot avoid it, and it happens sometimes.

– Is it worth it to give 150€ for a hotel in Santorini?
Usually, the level of service that you get from the hotel is much lower than the one you get at a Hilton chain hotel for the same price. But on the other side, it is expensive to keep a hotel in Santorini. The owners have to pay a lot for the land; they have to buy water as there are no natural water supplies in this volcano island, and the food is always imported. Santorini produces wines, tomatoes, and very few vegetables. The experience to stay at a hotel with this fantastic views of the caldera is one in a lifetime, so we recommend that you bite the bullet and spend some more money for your stay in Santorini. You will not regret it, and we can guarantee that you will break the "facebook likes" record once you start posting your photos on the social media.

– What about Car Parking for my rent-a-car?
You should always take care if there is a parking area for your rented car at the hotel you are staying. Santorini is busy in summer, and you might lose a lot of time to park, so always pay attention to that.

– What additional packages, trips, excursions, do hotels in Santorini offer?

Hotels in Santorini are affiliated with many tour operators, and they usually allow you to book different tours. The most common ones are a trip to the volcano and a trip around Santorini island with a boat. They also offer wine tours to the local wineries and scuba diving trips.

– How far is the airport from Fira, Oia, Imerovigli, Perissa?

Santorini is a small island, and you can transfer yourself from the airport to Fira in 15 minutes with a 15E taxi. Going to Oia will take 35 minutes.

– When Should I book my hotel to Santorini?

If you plan to visit Santorini in July and August, you should pre-book your hotel two months ago, to make sure that you get an excellent price for a nice hotel. Santorini has many hotels, and you will not suffer from finding a place to stay even in the busiest time. However, you may end up paying a lot of money if you book it at the last minute.

– When are the Busiest Months for Santorini?

August is the busiest month for Santorini. Then, it is July and September. Santorini has visitors starting from May until late October.

– When do Greeks visit Santorini?

The locals go to Santorini usually in July and August.

– When is it the best time to swim in Santorini?

July, August, and September are the best months for swimming in Santorini. June and October are usually ok, even though the sea gets colder than July and August.

What are the Best 4-stars and 5-stars Hotels to Stay in Santorini in each area?

If you decide to stay in Fira, you should check out the following hotels:

1. Cosmopolitan Suites Santorini: http://bit.ly/cosmopolitansantorini

2. Volcano View Hotel: http://bit.ly/volcanoview

3. Aigialos Niche Residence Suites

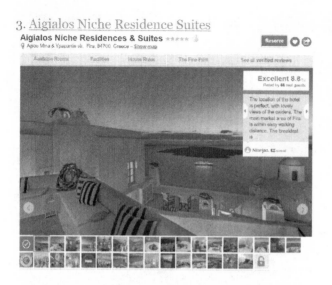

If you Decide to Stay in **Imerovigli** Village, you should try these hotels:

1. **Hotel Grace in Imerovigli, Santorini:** http://bit.ly/santorinigrace

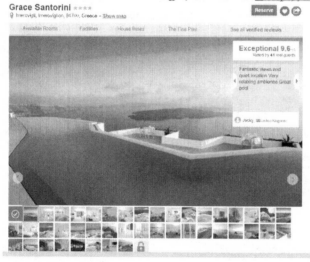

2. Hotel Vasilicos in Imerovigli, Santorini: http://bit.ly/vasilicos

3. Santorini Princess SPA hotel in Imerovigli, Santorini:

http://bit.ly/santoriniprincess

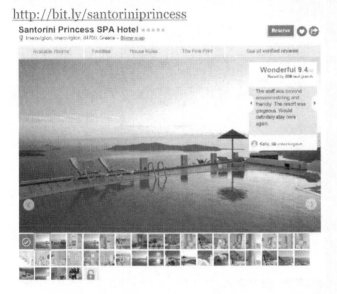

If you Decide to Stay in **Oia** Village, you should check out these hotels:

1. Katoikies hotel in Oia Village Santorini: http://bit.ly/hotelkatikies

2. Perivolas hotel in Oia Village, Santorini: http://bit.ly/peribolas

3. Kirini Suites and Spa Hotel in Oia Village, Santorini:

http://bit.ly/kirinisuites

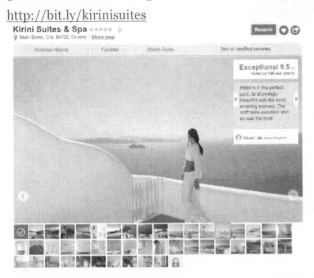

4. Ikies Traditional Houses in Oia Village, Santorini:

http://bit.ly/ikiessantorini

5. Santorini Secret Suites and Spa, Oia Village, Santorini:

http://bit.ly/secretsuites

If you decide to stay in **Perissa**, check out these hotels:

1. Resort Veggera, Perissa Village, Santorini:

http://bit.ly/veggerahotel

Fun Things to Do in Santorini

Santorini offers a wide variety of fun things to do, and we compiled a list of the seven most exciting activities to try in Santorini island:

#1 Enjoy the Santorini Sunset View from a Catamaran:
http://bit.ly/oceanvoyager

Most people go to Oia Village to enjoy the sunset. You can enjoy it even better if you go on a cruise around the island with a Catamaran. The cruise lasts 5 hours, and there is a barbecue prepared for you. The catamaran passes in front of the Red and the White Beaches, which is always a joy to swim in, especially when you jump from a boat.

The cost is rational, at 95 euros per person and you can book it at http://bit.ly/oceanvoyager . You will also get unlimited drinks - though not beer - so that you will have the chance to watch the sunset at Oia, as dizzy as possible. What's better than that?

#2 Go for a Wine Tour in Santorini: http://bit.ly/winetoursantorini

Santorini is a volcano island, and it is famous for its strange wines. Actually, the most famous wine from Santorini is called "Vinsanto, " and it is like a Porto - sweet with a peculiar accent. I will admit that most people have a love or hate relationship with the wines of Santorini. If you would like to find out in which camp you belong, you have to go on this four-hour tour, to the three best wineries in the island of Santorini.

The cost is around 90 euros per person, including transportation and pick-up from your hotel or from your cruise ship. You can book the four-hour wineries tour in Santorini, at http://bit.ly/winetoursantorini

#3 Tour the Volcano: http://bit.ly/volcanotoursantorini

You only cannot leave Santorini without going to the volcano...It has no bars, restaurants, swimming pools but how often do you walk on a Volcano in your home city in London or New York? You will even have the chance to see some steam getting out from the holes. No lava drama for all you adventurous photographers.

Just get this cruise, and go to swim in the thermal waters of the volcano (hint: if you are into intimate relationships or on your honeymoon, you should know that the smell from the thermal water leaves your body after a couple of days, and it is not the most pleasant one in the world..), walk on the volcano and get some lovely views of Santorini from the opposite side of the caldera.

You will be transferred from Santorini's main island to the volcano, with a traditional boat, which is called "Kaiki." It is a wooden boat that was used by the fishermen all over Greece for many years. This fun thing to do in Santorini will set you back only 40 euros per person and you can book it at http://bit.ly/volcanotoursantorini

#4 Go on a Helicopter Tour: http://bit.ly/helicoptertoursantorini

The world is always prettier when you see it from a chopper. Oh! And some Greek literature lessons. The world Helicopter is a Greek one, and it comes from the two Greek words "Elikas" and "pterugio" which mean, something that turns around and has wings.

So, if you want to make a marriage proposal on the air, just above the caldera of Santorini, or if you want to impress your significant other, or if no one loves you in this life, and you want to spoil yourself by consuming all your money, then you can just grab this helicopter tour.

It costs 1200 euros for 5 persons, so it is around 250 euros per person for half an hour. You can book it at http://bit.ly/helicoptertoursantorini . Of course, as always, the sunset in Santorini is like Coca-Cola: It matches well with everything. Yes, yes..you got it, you smart ladies...You can go on this helicopter tour during the sunset...

#5 Go on a Sailing Tour in Santorini: http://bit.ly/sailingtoursantorini

If you are the Marco Polo of tourists then you will want to grab a sailing boat and enjoy the perfect blue waters of Santorini.Hmm, well, they are a little bit dark blue (or even black) due to the volcanic stones, but that's another story.

So, back to our discussion, get this five-hour sailing tour around Santorini island. You will also get BBQ and lunch. To play the brave sailor, you will need to divorce yourself from 145 euros, which is 14 months of Netflix subscriptions. And now with the new Episodes of House of Cards hitting our screens, we know it will be a difficult decision to make. On the other side, you will get at least 1000 likes from posting your sailor-selfies on Facebook, which might be a thing for you. You can book it at http://bit.ly/sailingtoursantorini

#6 Go on a Santorini Cooking Class

You have seen it on TV, ate it at some miserable copycat "Greek" restaurants in other countries and now you have the chance of your life! The Greek food is among the best in the world, and you can learn how to cook and prepare it. This is what should be taught at Harvard and Universities around the world...no artificial intelligence, machine learning, and strange algorithmic theories... Don't worry, you will not need a Ph.D. to learn how to combine the tomato, with the onions and the feta cheese to make a perfect Greek salad. Get the crabs out of your pockets and pay 150 euros to get this cooking class (they also get you to some wineries to make it easier for you to forget the price). You can book it at http://bit.ly/foodtoursantorini

#7 Go for Sea Kayaking: http://bit.ly/kayaksantorini

Ok, we admit it. We hate sea kayaking, and whatever transportation vehicle does not have an engine and makes you sweat to move (hello bicycles...do you hear me?).

But we know that there are some strange persons on earth, that want to go on vacation and get as much tired as possible. So, for all you kayak aficionados out there, here is your chance.

You can kayak in the Natura protected area of Santorini, do some snorkeling and have fun. You can book it at http://bit.ly/kayaksantorini

Santorini Volcano: History, Tips before Going, How to Get There and the Best Boat and Catamaran Tours

A visit to Santorini is not complete unless you visit its famous volcano, the hot springs and enjoy swimming in the Red and White beach. Here is all you need to know before you plan your visit to the Santorini Volcano with a boat or catamaran tour.

- Where is the Santorini Volcano located?
The Santorini Volcano is located on the small volcanic island, called "Nea Kameni." It is opposite of the Santorini island and relatively close to it, as it takes around 10 minutes with a boat from Fira to reach the volcano, located at Nea Kameni. See the map below for a straightforward explanation of where the Santorini Volcano is located, in relation to Santorini, Thirasia, Palaia Kameni islands.

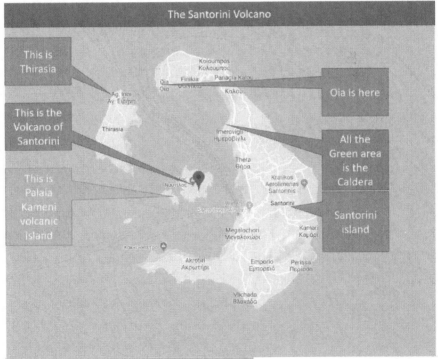

The Santorini Volcano - Where it is located

Santorini Volcano History

If you wonder how old the Santorini Volcano is, the answer is that it is 2 million years old. Yes, the very first volcanic eruptions in the area of Santorini, started 2 million years BC. Ok, that's a long time ago, so let's see what happened closer to our times.

The most crucial eruption of the Santorini Volcano has been 2000 years BC when the eruption created a huge earthquake which formed the crater in Santorini island and gave birth to the amazing caldera and some of the small volcanic islands next to it. The most important effect of this eruption, however, wasn't in Santorini island itself. It was in Crete island, which is around four hours by boat away from Santorini. The volcano explosion and the earthquake it created, has resulted in a huge tsunami, which hit the Crete island and has actually destroyed the most advanced civilization of Greece at that time. The Minoans. It was like an Aegean sea apocalypse.

Santorini Volcano Eruption History

So, when did the volcano erupt in Santorini? The most recent well-known eruptions of the Santorini Volcano have been in the years of 97 BC (created Palaia Kameni island), 1570 AD (created the Nea Kameni island), 1707 AD, 1866 AD, 1925 AD and 1956 AD. The lava magmas that came out from the eruptions once solidified have created the following volcanic islands: Thirassia, Aspronesi, Mikrà Kameni, Palea Kameni and Nea Kameni. All these islands are around the main Santorini Volcano and are facing the half-moon caldera of the Santorini island.

Will Santorini Volcano erupt again?

Most probably yes, but no one can predict the time. Don't worry though. The seismic activity that is evident before the volcanic eruptions will notify you well before, so you will have plenty of time to leave the island if you are soooo unlucky that a volcanic eruption occurs during your vacation to this wonderful place.

Santorini Volcano Last Eruption

A lot of people ask when was the last eruption of Santorini. The answer is that the last eruption of the Santorini Volcano took place in 1956 and destroyed part of the Imerovigli village. And if you wonder if the volcano in Santorini is still active, the answer is that yes, it is still active but in a dormant mode. So, no need to worry that is going to erupt while you visit Santorini. Volcanos don't erupt from one moment to the other, so in the worst case scenario, they will be plenty of time to deal with the unexpected.

Santorini Volcano - How to get there

So, how do you get to the Santorini Volcano, in Nea Kameni volcanic island? There is no public boat service that connects Fira, Imerovigli, Oia or other parts of Santorini with Nea Kameni, as the latter is a small uninhabited island and there is no reason for a public transportation to existing. That means that you have to get a boat tour to go the Santorini Volcano from Santorini island.

Santorini Volcano - Hot Springs Information & Tips (don't dive before you read this)

A popular stop for many tours going from Santorini to the Santorini Volcano in Nea Kameni is the area of the Hot Springs. This area is in a small cave next to Nea Kameni, where the boat stops and you can jump in the water from the boat and swim in the thermal waters. Now, you have to be careful with swimming in the hot springs. The reason is that the water smells sulphur, so it smells really bad. And it is not clear, but muddy. Your skin and your clothes will smell bad for some hours and even days. Most probably, you will have to through away your swimming suit due to the stains it is going to have from the chemicals in the water, as you will not want to wear it again. So, don't go to the Hot Springs with your best expensive swimming suit but get another, old and cheap one that you might get rid of easily after the boat trip.

Santorini Volcano Tours

You can get a Santorini Volcano Tour from Fira, Perissa, Kamari or even other places in the Santorini island, as most of the tours offer a free pick-up and return from your hotel. The cheaper tours will not do it obviously, so you will have to transfer to the departure area. As said, you cannot get a Santorini to Volcano visit without the tour. The catamarans usually depart from Vlychada village, outside of Fira.

Here are the most popular tour routes that exist from Santorini to the Volcano:

Fira to Hot Springs to Volcano and back to Fira. Some Tours include the Red and White beach.

This is a popular route for boats and catamarans that they usually pick you up at your hotel, leave from Fira, go to the Hot Springs at Palaia Kameni island, then visit the Volcano at the Nea Kameni island and return to Fira. Typically, these tours last four to five hours and leave you time for swimming and hiking in the volcano.

Here is the map with the most usual stops of the boat tours:

The best Santorini Volcano boat or catamaran tours are:

Santorini Sailing DreamCatcher, 5-hour Sailing Tour in the Volcano: http://bit.ly/2JlHmxu

Santorini Volcano Tour - Dreamcatcher

This tour lasts 5 hours. They pick you up from your hotel, it takes you to the thermal springs, then to the volcano and they cook a bbq for you. It allows time for snorkeling and swimming in the hot springs and a couple of other bays. It costs around 100 euros per person. This tour uses a catamaran, which is an interesting experience by itself. Check prices at http://bit.ly/2JlHmxu

The Santorini Catamaran Red Cruise

Santorini Volcano Tour - Red Catamaran

The tour with this catamaran lasts for five hours and they pick you up from your hotel, with a minibus. It will take you to the Santorini caldera, then to the Red and White beach for some swimming, then to the Hot Springs and finally to the Volcano. It also offers beverages and a bbq with pork or chicken. The cost is around 90 euros per person.

The maximum persons on the catamaran are around 50 to 55, so it's not a private experience. Make sure to bring your own towels, as they are not provided by the tour operators. Book it at http://bit.ly/oceanvoyager

4- hour Tour to the Volcano in Nea Kameni and the Hot Springs

Santorini Volcano Tour - Boat Tour

This is a cheaper tour, which costs around 30 euros per person. It lasts four hours and it will get you to the hot springs, then to the Volcano and back to Fira in Santorini island. The boat used is a simpler, standard one and not a catamaran. They will also pick you up from the hotel you stay at (Kamari, Fira, and Perissa) but there is no lunch or bbq included in the tour. You can book it at http://bit.ly/2vFD1mQ

Semi-Private Boat Tour to the Volcano and the Hot Springs with a Luxury Catamaran

Santorini Volcano Tour - Semi-Private Catamaran Tour

Again, this tour lasts about five hours. They pick you up from your hotel, and the catamaran will get you to the hot springs and to the Volcano. They will offer towels, so you don't have to bring your own. They also offer unlimited wines and beverages and a greek buffet on board. There will around 15 to 18 people on board, so don't expect that semi-private means under ten people on the catamaran. This tour costs around 170 euros per person and has great reviews. You can book it at http://bit.ly/2Hpv7DK

Santorini Gems: Small Group (semi-private) sailing cruise on a Catamaran :

Santorini Volcano Tour - Santorini Gems

This tour is on a catamaran which stops at three sites for you to swim. It lasts for five hours and it takes you to the Red Beach, then to the White beach, to the Hot Springs, and to the Volcano. It offers barbeque, drinks, wifi onboard, snorkeling equipment and they pick you up from your hotel and return you back. It costs around 140 euros per person. Book it at http://bit.ly/2qWQxxV

Perissa Beach Santorini – All you Need to Know about the most famous beach of Santorini

Perissa beach in Santorini is the most famous beach on the island for a good reason: It is a long, black and sandy, volcanic beach, unlike anything you have swum into in your life. Here is what you need to know about the Perissa Beach.

Where is Perissa Beach?

Perissa beach is located in the southeast part of Santorini, 12 KMs away from the main village of Santorini, which is called "Fira". You will need around 25 minutes to drive from Fira to Perissa beach and around 40 minutes to get from Oia to Perissa beach. Have a look below for a better understanding of the location of Perissa beach.

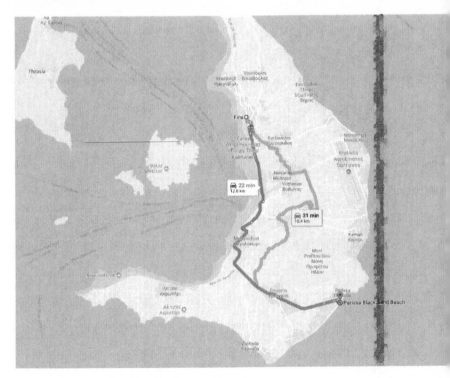

How Does Perissa Beach Look Like?

The Perissa Beach is around 4kms long, and 50 meters wide, with black sand. You will see many sunbeds on the beach, and there are some empty spots if you carry your own sun equipment, such as umbrellas.

- Is There a Perissa Town in Santorini?
Yes, indeed, there is a town called Perissa in Santorini and the beach belongs to this small town.

Perissa Beach Santorini: Things to Do
A few of the best things to do in Perissa beach are the following:
-Relax on the beach by renting a sunbed and an umbrella. The cost starts from 7 euros and gets up to 10 euros for a set of two sunbeds and an umbrella, for the whole day. There are some beach bars that offer the sunbeds for free as long as you order food and drinks from them, but most beach bars tend to rent them. Also, the beach bars will offer you free wi-fi. Many beach bars are slow on the orders and you may have to wait for 30 minutes to get your food, so please be patient.
-Do some water sports, as there is a dedicated water sports center in Perissa with many fun activities to do.
-During the afternoon, have a couple of drinks in one of the famous Perissa beach restaurants or bars, such as "Chilly" or "Wet".
-Enjoy the nightlife in Perissa beach bars, in one of the late afternoon parties they organize.

How is the Water and the Sea in Perissa Beach?
The sea is quite cold until May and it gets warmer from June until the end of September. The sea is not that swallow, but you can walk for around 10-15

meters inside the sea. There are usually no big waves, and it is quite calm. I you have children you should always be very careful in this beach, as it is crowded and it's easy to lose sight of your kids.

Moreover, be careful with the sand on the beach. As it is black, it attracts a lot of sun's energy and it gets extremely hot. Always wear your flip-flops when moving around.

How to Get to Perissa Beach from Fira or Oia
If you don't have a car, then you should get a public bus from Fira or Oia, which ends its trip to Perissa village and it will usually stop right on the beach.

1st Day in Santorini: Arrival, Fira, Firostefani, Imerovigli, Oia, Kamari Beach and Top Things to Do

07:50am. Arrival at the Santorini International Airport
The airport of Santorini is a tiny airport which is located north of the village of *Kamari*, and it is about 6 km southeast of downtown Thira. Thira or Fira is the name of the capital city (actually it is a village) of Santorini island. **Website:** http://www.santoriniairportguide.com

08:00am. Take the luggage and go through the passport control.
Tip: It does not take more than 3 minutes to get your luggage and exit the passport control. Santorini's airport is a tiny airport.

08:05am. Take a **taxi** from the airport to the city center, to reach the recommended hotel (12 min distance).

Our hotel is at Firostefani village- which is a 3' distance from Fira.
Cost: 120€/ double room

Firostefani is only 1km from Fira, and it is a great village where you can find several walking paths that lead to the Caldera, to enjoy the unique view that Santorini island has to offer. Why do we recommend that you stay in Firostefani village and not in Fira or Oia village? Because Firostefani is in the highest part of the island, offering a better view to the caldera, it is quieter than the hyper-busy Fira village – while it is conveniently located close to it.

View from Firostefani

08:20am. Accommodate yourself in the hotel and then start discovering Firostefani village and the nearby villages including Imerovigli and Oia village.

Start your day visiting the famous Santorini's villages with the spectacular Cycladic architecture and the excellent view of the Aegean Sea and the volcano. Enjoy your walk at Firostefani. Then, take a taxi or rent a bike or a car and walk to Imerovigli village (1,5km from Firostefani) and then drive to the Oia village (10km from Firostefani).

On the side of the Caldera, the view of the volcanic rocks and the volcano is astonishing, while on the opposite side you will admire the Aegean Sea. From this point on you will drive near the impressive Black and Red mountains. At the entrance of Oia village, you will find a sign showing a right turn to *Finikia and Baxedes*. Driving straight ahead you will enter Oia. Oia a very famous place for its sunset.

Many couples are visiting Oia village during the sunset time, to pass some romantic time, watching the sun go down. Passing through the village, you will find access points to the main pedestrian street offering a fantastic view to the Caldera and the neighborhoods of Oia. There are several parking lots which also serve as the bus stations.

Imerovigli Village

Oia Village

10:30am. Coffee at 'Melenio Pastry Shop'- Oia Village
Enjoy your coffee with some local handmade sweets at the balcony of the café, which offers a fantastic view.
Don't forget to taste some *"galaktoboureko"* (a sweet with white cream inside), chocolate pie or *"baklavas"* (the Greek version).

12.30pm. Lunch at 'Anogi' Tavern at the Imerovigli Village
This tavern-restaurant is located in the Main Street between Fira and Oia village.
Tel.: +30 22860 21285
This tavern offers a tasteful local cuisine with a modern sensation
Tip: Order the *tomato balls* (*"tomato keftedes"* in Greek) and the split peas of Santorini (called "fava" in Greek).
Expected Cost: Around 20€ per person, with a glass of wine.

14.30pm. Go to Kamari beach and relax under the sun.
The beach has black sand and clean waters. You can enjoy your drink there, in any one of the plenty beach bars that you will find nearby.

Kamari Beach
Kamari, a 5km beach with black stones, is one of the most famous beaches of the island. At the south side of the beach, you may see the 'Mesa Vouno' (the inside Mountain) of the ancient Santorini. You may also see many airplanes that are passing very close to the beach, as the airport is very close to Kamari village.

43

17:30pm Return to the hotel and get some rest.

19.00pm Enjoy the Sunset in Oia village.
In case you are a couple or a sunset hunter, do not miss this magic moment and unique sunset view. You need to protect your eyes if you are going to watch the sunset so you could use your sunglasses and a glass of something good to drink while watching the sun shyly dip its underbelly into the sea! Don't look directly into the sun.

The Sunset at Oia Village is a Popular Touristic Attraction

Tip: Be ready to secure a good spot well ahead of the sunset – at least a hour ahead. Hordes of tourists go to bask in the warm sunshine. You have find the perfect spot, fend off a hundred fellow sunset gazers and then t very hard to crop them out of your photos.

20:45pm. Go to Fira Village and enjoy a crepe at 'Creme de la Crepe.'
Try it either with cheese, mushrooms, and ham or sweet with white chocolate and strawberries.
Crème de la Crepe: Georgiou Nomikou Street, Fira, Santorini, tel. +(3(22860 36463

21.30pm. Discover Fira Village.
Great white paths with many local shops and restaurants

Fira Village

Tip: if you are visiting Santorini during the high season (June-August) you should know that the central square at Fira is closed for vehicles, and you will have to take a detour if you are driving a car.

22.30pm. Enjoy your cocktail at Franco's Bar, one the oldest and most famous bars of the island
Website: http://www.francos.gr/
Drink the famous 'Maria Kallas,' a cocktail prepared with champagne.
Tip: It is a bit expensive bar (a cocktail cost is 13-15€) but the view, and the cocktails are breathtaking. So, it is the fantastic view that you are paying for and not so much the cocktails.

12.30am. Return to the hotel and get some rest.

Santorini 1st Day Map

Below you can get the map of all the suggested activities for your first day
Santorini. This map is accessible as a Google Maps format so that you ca
quickly zoom in and view it on any device, tablet, laptop or smartphone yo
might have. Just click on the photo or on the link below to access it.

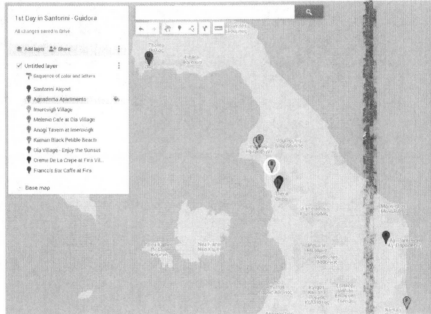

Get this Map Online in Google Maps Format: http://bit.ly/2HTCmDc

2nd Day in Santorini: Volcano & Caldera Tour, Hot Spring, Thirasia, Oia and Fira Nightlife

09.00am **Enjoy your breakfast at your hotel and then get ready for the volcano and caldera guided tour.**

Tip: If you go to Santorini from May to September, take your swimming suit, a water bottle, your hat, sneakers and certainly lots of sunscreens. In case you are not in a good physical condition, please avoid this route, as the path when you are at the volcano is uphill, and the ground is unstable.

10.00am **Depart from the hotel and Discover the Volcano New Kameni, the hot springs, and the Thirasia.**

Many boats can take you to the volcano and Thirasia. Most of them depart either from the old port of Fira, which is called "Gialos," or from the new one, which is called "Athinio."

It is better that you take the boat from the old port of Fira, Gialos. We suggest the tour operators called *Volcano Tours*, as with them it is easy to pre-book this trip many days before going to the island. Go to the following website to pre-book your tour: http://aegeantraveller.gr/tours-volcano.html.

It is not that vital to pre-book since there are quite a few tour operators, so if you would like to decide whether you want to go to the volcano, while you are in Santorini's island, you could search for tour operators while you are in Fira
If you want to have the volcano and Caldera guided tour, to swim at the hot springs, go to Thirassia and then to Oia, take the boat that departs at 10.30am- it *costs 26€ per person.*

This tour is extraordinary as you will have the chance to explore Santorini from a different perspective. You will have the opportunity to walk to the rim of the volcanic crater at New Kameni.

47

Nea Kameni (Volcano)

Then, the boat will take you to Palaia Kameni (old Kameni) and the therm
springs. The captain will drop anchor in the shallows, where you can take
swim. The waters are yellowish and five degrees hotter than the rest of tl
sea.

Palaia Kameni-Hot Springs

Tip. The smell of your body, after the swimming at the thermal springs, will not leave immediately, and I would say that smells really ugly. This is because the water has sulfite salts due to the emissions of the volcano.

Next stop will be at the picturesque islet of Thirasia and its village, "*Manolas,*" at the top of Caldera. At the end of the tour, you will have a small stop at the marvelous village of Oia.

Thirasia Island

Tip. In case you are an amateur or professional diver, bear in mind that the great volcanic eruptions that shook the island over the centuries have created a magnificent underwater scenery, giving scuba diving lovers endless options for never ending drop-offs around the Caldera and the volcanic islets. The promontory of Trypiti in Therasia, the shipwreck in Taxiarhis, Palia Kameni, the Armeni near Oia (for wall dives) or the area of Adiavati near Akrotiri are great diving spots. However, this tour will not permit you to discover this scenery.

Santorini Dive Center is one of the best centers that will help you to discover the hidden treasures of Santorini.

Santorini Dive Center, Perissa Beach Road. Tel.: +30 2286 083190
Here are the costs: http://www.divecenter.gr

16.30pm. Return to the old port of Fira, Gialos, and go to the hotel to g
some rest.

19.00pm. **Dinner at 'Aktaion'** –Firostefani square

Aktaion Tavern

This tavern serves some excellent Greek food. Try the grilled white eggpla
trilogy, the homemade traditional pasta 'Makarounes' with caper leave
capers, and garlic, the homemade *Mousakas* with vegetables from Santori
and the fried cod fish fillet with beetroot puree. Here is the menu:
http://www.aktaionsantorini.com/restaurant/menu

20.30pm. **Time for 'loukoumades,'** the traditional donuts with hon
and cinnamon, white chocolate or ice-cream at *Lukumum* - Fira
Info: "Lukumum"- Danezi Street, Fira Tel.+30 2286 02467
https://www.facebook.com/Lukumumsantorini/

21.30pm. **Enjoy your cocktail at the famous 'Tango' bar at Fira**.
serves great cocktails such as Mojito, Mai Tai, Mimosa, and Bellini. It al
provides a great view to Santorini.

12.30pm. **It' s time for dancing at *Koo club*.**

Koo Club

Nightlife in Santorini is a remarkable experience. Koo Club is ideal for partying or just chilling out with a cocktail. Great music and drinks!
Koo Club, Fira, tel. +30 2286 022025

03.00am. **Return to the hotel and rest.**

Santorini 2nd Day – Map

Below you can find the map with all the suggested places for your second day in Santorini. You can click on the linkto see it in the online format of Google maps so that you can easily navigate when you are in Santorini.

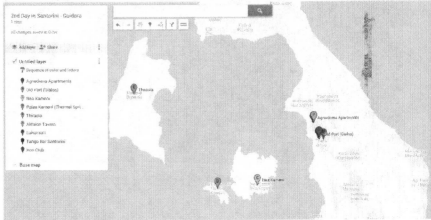

Click Here to Get this Map Online: http://bit.ly/2KbiCcG

3d Day in Santorini: Akrotiri, Perivolos, Vlychada and Return

This is the itinerary for your third day in Santorini, with all the suggested activities to follow.

09.30am Breakfast at the hotel

10.30am Check out from the hotel. Departure for the prehistoric settlement of **Akrotiri,** the most prominent archaeological site in Santorini.

Akrotiri Archaeological Site

The first habitation of Akrotiri dates back from the Late Neolithic times (at least the 4th millennium BC). Its large extent of the settlement, the great drainage system, the sophisticated buildings with the extraordinary wall paintings and furniture, testify its significant development. Read about its history at http://odysseus.culture.gr/

Wall-Painting in Akrotiri

How to Go to Akrotiri:
Distance from Firostefani: 12km-around 20' drive
Take the 'Fira's Straight' road with direction to the port. The view
exceptional during the whole route, as you drive parallel to Caldera.

Firstly, you will pass by the old mines. This is a good chance to take sor
pictures of the volcano. After 3,6 km from Fira, ascend to the right to rea
an intersection from which the road on the left leads to Pyrgos village, a
the straight one leads to the intersection to the port, Megalohori, Akrot
and the beaches of the southeast and southwest part of the island. Headi
for Akrotiri, on your right a sign that indicates the road to the Athinios po
and enters the area of Megalohori. There are vineyards on both sides of t
main road.

After 1,5 km, away from the sign to Athinios, you will see another sign th
indicates the way to Megalohori village. Drive on the main road and just aft
Megalohori makes a right turn to Akrotiri (there is a sign). In about 4 km y
will arrive at the settlement of Akrotiri. Pass through it and follow t
signage that will drive you to the parking outside the archaeological area.
the end of the road, you may see the red beach.

Tip: One of the biggest problems of the island is that it misses of signs at t
roads. Do not miss to use your GPS or ask for one in case you rent a car.

Useful Information:
The Archaeological Site of Akrotiri is open to visitors from 10:00 am to 17:00 pm.

Tickets Costs: Full Price Ticket: 12€ per person, Reduced Price Ticket: 6€ per person
Akrotiri Excavations Tel: +30 22860 81366

Reduced Admission for:
- Greek citizens and citizens of other Member - States of the €pean Union aged over 65 years old by showing their ID card or passport.
- Students of Higher Education Institutes and equivalent Schools from countries outside the EU by showing their student ID
- The accompanying parents on educational visits to elementary schools

Free Admission for:
- Cultural Card Holders
- Journalists with their professional card
- Members of Associations of Friends of Museums and Archaeological sites- they need to demonstrate their membership card at the entrance
- ICOM-ICOMOS members
- Persons who accompany blinds and disabled
- The escorting teachers of schools and institutions
- The official guests of Greek government
- The tourist guides who demonstrate their Ministry of Culture and Tourism professional identity
- University and Technological Educational Institutes students or equivalent schools of Member-States of the European Union
- Young people under the age of 18- they have to demonstrate their passport to confirm their age

Free Admission Days:
- 6 March (in memory of Melina Merkouri)
- 5 June (International Environment Day)
- 18 April (International Monuments Day)
- 18 May (International Museums Day)
- The last weekend of September annually (€pean Heritage Days)
- National Holidays (28th of October and 25th of March)
- Every 1st Sunday from 1 November to 31 March

Tip: In case you want to taste or buy some traditional wines of Santorini, there are two wineries which are called "Boutaris" and "Gavalas" wineries, which are located within the Megalohori village.

13.00pm Swim at one of the most spectacular beaches of Santorini, th famous **Red Beach.**

You will be impressed by the unique landscape of red and black volcan rocks from the headland.

You can access the beach either by a boat that departs from the Akrotiri po or you can park your car at the parking space and walk all the way down which is a 2 minutes' distance. As you gradually get down to the red beac you will have the chance to admire the different colorings of the cliffs. Yc may find sunbeds and umbrellas that cover the dark sand.
If you like snorkeling, this is a perfect place to discover a bed plenty interesting rocks.

Danger: Please be careful with this beach! The rocks could easily fall in case of a small earthquake. Try to be in a safe place.

The famous "Red Beach."

Tip: The small size of the beach creates a much crowded atmospher especially during July and August.

14.30pm.: Lunch at the Cave of Nikolas-Akrotiri, **Cave of Nikolas Tavern**
Info: +30 22860 82303, http://www.thecave-ofnikolas.gr/en

This is one of the best taverns of the island if you like dining next to the sea. The owners use their vegetables from their field for their dishes. Mrs. Margarita, the cook, prepares the best tomato balls of the island. The homemade moussakas with white eggplant, the special tomato ball with cod fish inside, and the fresh fishes are very tasteful and highly recommended.

Cave of Nikolas Tavern

16.30pm. It's time to discover another beautiful beach of the island- the **Perivolos beach.**

Perivolos Beach

The beach, located only 3km from Perissa beach and 10km from Akrotiri, has built its reputation thanks to its sparkling azure blue waters and its dark sand. Perivolos is surely one of the most well-organized beaches of the island, offering water sports facilities, such as windsurfing, jet ski, and scuba diving. On the beachfront, there are numerous beach bars, taverns, and pubs that serve local delicacies and drinks. There you may sip your cocktail at 'Chili' beach bar and relax listening to the mainstream hits.

If you rent an umbrella and two seats, you should expect to pay around 10 for the set, for the whole day.

19.00pm. Time for Greek traditional fish dishes at 'Psaraki' tavern Vlichada.
Psaraki Tavern: Tel. +30 22860 82783, http://www.topsaraki.gr

Psaraki Tavern

At 'Psaraki' you can taste excellent seafood dishes, with a view to the small port of Vlichada. Fish soup, homemade vine leaves stuffed with rice, grilled sardines stuffed with herbs and shrimps "saganaki" with feta and ouzo are some of the specialties of the tavern. You may also taste some of the local Santorini wines and beers.

21.00pm. Departure **for the airport-** 12km from Vlychada.
Take the road that goes from Fira to Perissa. It is about a 20' drive.

3d Day in Santorini – Map

We have created an online google maps with all the suggested places and sights of your third day in Santorini, so that you can navigate easily to them.

Click on the link to view it in Google Maps format: http://bit.ly/2Fgfatr

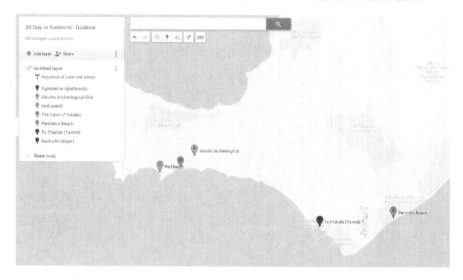

How to Eat Like a Greek: 21 Dishes to Try While You are in Santorini

This is a section in our guide for the food lovers; that is going to explain step by-step, how to make the most of your culinary experience in Greece. Greece offers fantastic food, with local vegetables, cheeses, and meat. Although the menu could be huge and cover every passion you may have, here is a list of the must-try dishes in Greece.

Try these amazing Greek Food Starters:
-Tzatziki (yogurt with cucumber and garlic)

Tzatziki is a Greek sauce that you can try with grilled meats or as a dip with bread. Tzatziki is made of strained yogurt which comes from sheep or goat milk, and it is mixed with garlic, salt, cucumbers and olive oil. You may add mint, dill or parsley. Try it with bread, fried potatoes, and grilled meat or grilled fish. And get a mint for your breadth afterward

-Melitzanosalata (eggplant salad).

This is made with eggplants, olive oil, garlic and sometimes with Greek cheese (feta cheese) on top, split into pieces. Try with grilled meat or fried fish.

- Ntolmadakia (grape leaves stuffed with rice)

A great starter that you can also find in Turkey. It is made of grape leaves, stuffed with rice and sometimes with minced meat. Try it with tzatziki (Yes, Tzatziki is like the Coke – you can combine it with almost everything!)

-Fried potatoes (Greek, French fries)

Make sure you get the fresh Greek, french fries. Some restaurants serve pre-fried ones, which are nowhere close to the original ones. Ask before you order.

- Greek Salad

This is the most famous dish of Greece. Fantastic salad. Particularly in the summer. Cucumber, tomato, Greek feta cheese, onions, pepper and olive oil. Secret tip: Take a piece of bread and make a "dive" as it is called in Greece, in the olive oil, which carries all the flavors of the vegetables.

Main Courses
- Souvlaki (sticks with pork meat, grilled)

Try them with Greek French fries, tzatziki, and pita. And a Greek salad.

- Paidakia (lamb chops)
These are grilled lamb chops, just with lemon. You know that lamb has a peculiar odor and taste that is quite different from the pork or vein. Some love them; some hate them.

- Mousaka

A plate of Turkish origin, with eggplant, bechamel, mince, and sometimes other vegetables. Try one piece. No more. Greeks combine this with a piece of "feta" cheese.

- Pastitsio

Pasta, with mince and bechamel. Fantastic in the summer, together with Greek feta an a Greek salad. Make sure it is freshly cooke and served. You can combine it with a piece of "feta" cheese. Expect to pay around 7 euros for each piece of Pastitsio.

- Fish (e.g. ask for Barbounia, Koutsomoures, which are red fish fried)

Greeks eat a lot of small, fried fish when going out in tavernas. The cheapest one is th fried sardines and the most tasty ones, albei more expensive, are the "red fish" with the names of "barbounia" and "koutsomoures". Ask if they are fresh and order some of them You just pour some lemon on them and you can combine them with some fried calamari, a grilled octopus and a Greek salad.

- Stuffed calamari

There are several different ways to order the calamari in Greece. The two most popular ones are to get it fried and to get it stuffed with rice and Greek cheese. Always ask if th calamari is fresh; the frozen one is also very tasty but you should not pay a frozen calamari as if it was fresh.

- Grilled Octopus

In Greece, you can order the octopus either boiled or grilled. The boiled one is softer to chew but the grilled one is more tasty.

- Spaghetti with Lobster (*Astakomakaronada* in Greek)

This is one of the most famous dishes during the summer in Greece and especially in the Greek islands. There are many ways to cook the lobster when you combine it with Spaghetti. Usually, the cook it with a red sauce from fresh tomatoes and some herbs. It is an expensive dish to try, but it worth's it! One kg of lobster with spaghetti costs around 80 to 100 euros. Of course, this is more than enough for two people and you should not order other starters. Maybe just a salad with herbs.

Desserts You Can Try in Greece
Galaktompoureko (milk pie)

This is a milk pie and it is a great way to start your day with a piece of "Galaktompoureko".

Revani

The most famous place for Revani in Greece is a town in northern Greece, called "Veroia." However, you can enjoy this in many places all over Greece. It is like a cake, with extra syrup and a light flavor of orange. Amazing and light! You can combine it with vanilla ice-cream.

63

Greek Halva

A Greek sweet made with tahini and sugar. The most famous Greek halvas is from "Kosmidis", which you can find in many deli shops. Halvas comes in different flavors, including chocolate and cacao.

Ice-cream (Try *kaimaki* flavor and add "Vyssino."

Kaimaki flavor is a little bit like vanilla with twist.

Baklavas Sweet

This sweet comes from Turkey. It is delicious and it is quite sweet.

You should also try Greek coffees: Try freddo espresso, freddo cappuccino, and Greek frappe.

Freddo Espresso: A top Invention in Greece, since 2000!

The top invention of the 2000 decade in Greece! Even Italians want to copy this to their country. You get a hot espresso (double one usually), and you put some sugar in it. Then you place an ice-cube, and you mix it until it cools down. Then you add the ice cubes, and you enjoy.

Freddo Cappuccino

One of the top inventions in Greece! You will not find this easily in other countries, not even in Italy! In Greece, people don't like the hot coffees in the summer. Moreover, Greeks don't like that much the very sweet cold coffees that Starbucks or other similar chains create for the season.

So, one of the top innovations of the last 15 years in Greece, was the Freddo Cappucino! This is based on the hot espresso coffee, and you add some sugar and one ice cube, and you mix it. After that, you add the ice cubes. Moreover, you get milk with full fat, and you hit it until it becomes more "foamy" and you add it on top of the coffee you created. The result is the following – usually, people adore it! If you don't like the milk, you can get it just with coffee and without any milk – in that case, it is called "Freddo Espresso."

The best coffee chains in Greece to try that is "Everest," where you can get it in Brazilian or Arabica coffee selection and "Grigoris." Of course, this is a mainstream coffee in Greece, and you will find it almost everywhere nowadays.

Greek Frappe

Italians are great in hot coffees like espresso and cappuccino. Greeks are great in two kinds of coffees: The hot one, which is called "the Turkish coffee – or Greek coffee" and the cold ones. The first cold coffee invented in Greece by Nestle, back in the 1980s is the "frappe coffee." This is a strong coffee that has a special way to prepare. You get some Nestle frappe coffee sliced beans, and you mix them with sugar. Then you put some water and you start to shake it, or you mix it with a hand-mixer. Then you add the ice cubes. The result is a cold, tasty coffee, which is called "frappe." It also gets high foam on top of it!

It's a strong coffee, and you have to drink it slowly. Otherwise, you may get an issue with your stomach. Don't drink more than one per day if you are not used to it – otherwise, you will not sleep during the night.

This coffee is not that mainstream anymore in Greece. The young generation snobs it and prefers to drink the Freddo Espresso or Freddo Cappuccino, which are based on the Italian espresso coffee. We also prefer Freddo Espresso to the Greek Frappe.

What could you ask more? Simply a fantastic kitchen, probably one of the best five on earth, together with Italian, Mexican, French and Spanish cuisine. Enjoy!

The Best Tours to Book in Santorini

Here is the information on the best tours to book while you are in Santorini. The best site to book your tours and get some decent discounts is GetyourGuide (http://bit.ly/2JpeoNi)

The best tours are:

#1 Santorini Half-Day Small Group and Private Wine Tour:
http://bit.ly/2KbXove
A four-hour tour that gets you to 3 wineries, in the countryside of Santorini. Wine tasting tips from experts.

#2 Santorini 5-hour Catamaran Cruise: http://bit.ly/2vGVTSF
The Catamaran will get you to the Red Beach and the White Beach to swim and snorkel. You see the sunset from the catamaran and enjoy a bbq dinner of grilled pork and Greek salad. Finally, it gets you through the Caldera and lets you swim in the hot spring waters.

#3 Santorini Volcano Tour and Oia Sunset Cruise:
http://bit.ly/2JnrA5s
This is an 8-hour tour which gets you to the volcano, to the small island called "Thirassia" and then to Oia village to see the sunset.

#4 Santorini Cooking Class and Wine-Tasting Tour:
http://bit.ly/2qZhjoy
You get to visit some wineries in Santorini and learn how to cook Greek food from a Greek Chef. You get to try nine different Greek wines and you will a full dinner is also included.

#5 Santorini Full Day Private Tour: http://bit.ly/2qUhBwO

#6 Santorini 7 Hour Volcano Adventure with Cruise:
http://bit.ly/2HYFICH

#7 Helicopter Tour in Santorini: http://bit.ly/2Hr9Sx7
You fly with a chopper over Santorini, for 20, 40 or 60 minutes.

Thank you!

Thank you for choosing this Guidora Guide for Santorini. We hope that it
going to help you to make the most out of your stay in Santorini. If you ha
any feedback on how to improve, or if you just had a great time in Istanb
and you'd like to share that, just send us an email to admin@guidora.com.

Have an amazing time in Santorini!

Your friends at Guidora.